Aileron

Also by Geraldine Connolly

Hand of the Wind
Province of Fire
Food for the Winter
The Red Room (chapbook)

Aileron

by

Geraldine Connolly

Terrapin Books

© 2018 by Geraldine Connolly
Printed in the United States of America
All rights reserved.
No part of this book may be reproduced in any manner, except for brief quotations embodied in critical articles or reviews.

Terrapin Books
4 Midvale Avenue
West Caldwell, NJ 07006

www.terrapinbooks.com

ISBN: 978-0-9982159-9-0
LCCN: 2017963949

First Edition

Cover art: *Inspissated,* by LM Grimes, 2017
www.lewismarkgrimes.com

for my granddaughters
Adela, Keira, Porter, and Garland

Contents

Aileron   7

I

Fable of the Good Daughter   11
Legacy   12
Hunger   14
Dining Room Overlooking the Garden
   (The Breakfast Room)   15
Childhood Play   16
Blackberries   18
Ontario   19
The Great Lake   20
Buckeye   22
Cinder   23
October: The Farm Is Gone   24
Freight   25
Seckel Pear   26

II

Dear Tomato   29
Kindergarten   30
River of Mantises   31
Montana   33
Thinking About St. Agnes   34
Avalanche   36
Packing Up to Leave   37
Ode to My Lost Quickness   38
When I See Crows   39
The First Time   40
Bethel Road   41

III

Being a Female   45
I Am Tired of Being a Wife   46

Seeking the Father . . . 47
Sisters . . . 48
The Smell of Workmen . . . 50
A Memory . . . 52
The Right Words . . . 53
Tambourines . . . 54
Protea . . . 55
The Hardware of the Brain . . . 56
Surrender . . . 58
A Long Marriage . . . 59
Every Manner of Crooked Stem and Thorn . . . 60
The Border . . . 62
Kingfisher . . . 63
My Granddaughter's Face . . . 64
Sixtieth Birthday . . . 65
Sea of Cortez . . . 66

IV

Leaving Montana . . . 69
Ode to a Mesquite Tree . . . 70
My Self-Confidence . . . 71
Out of Balance . . . 72
Sunlight Passes . . . 73
One by One: Gambel's Quail . . . 74
Empty Storefront . . . 76
Mission of San Xavier del Bac: Waiting
    for Signs of Providence . . . 77
Shirt . . . 78
Soon . . . 79
Boxcars . . . 80
Amulet . . . 81
Happiness: A Painting from the Lost World . . . 82

Acknowledgments . . . 85
About the Author . . . 87

An aileron *(French for "little wing" or "fin")* is a hinged flight control surface usually forming part of the trailing edge of each wing of a fixed-wing aircraft.

Aileron

Once I rode a one-eyed horse
to a tree house in the forest.

Once I was a child spreading
tomorrow's clean clothes

over the back of a chair.
I greeted three pheasants at dawn

escaping the mist of a cold river.
Once the minutes flew like hummingbirds

buzzing over speedwell.
I floated in a wood canoe through

mill town haze and green banks.
Once she was breathing in my sleep,

kicking the flesh under my breastbone.
Once the waves rose high and cold,

the smoky silt stung my skin.
What was beneath terrified me

and my dreams made me swoon:
swollen grandmothers rising,

balloons into limbo, the part
that dragged, the part that lifted.

Did I count my sins?
Did I sin?

I counted my breaths, I counted my steps.
I numbered the days toward escape.

I burned candles for the lives
I had not lived.

The wind was always blowing me backward,
interring my course until I deflected.

Childhood passed.
I became feathers swiveling,

always the gravity escaping, eluding,
memory the weight of stones.

Now I explode into the unknown,
restless, on fire with fast air.

The air divides as I pull up to climb,
to turn and tilt, to stay aloft.

Fable of the Good Daughter

Once a milkweed, once a daisy,
once I was a pleasant, gauzy girl.

I raked hay and weeded the garden.
I had to raise myself,
wake myself, cook and prepare
for the day. I remember wanting
more time, more affection,
expecting to inherit the farm, until
the acres were sold and devoured
by trucks and chemicals.

Once like a flower I wanted to be good.
Once I prayed and obeyed.
But something must always happen.
Say, a betrayal.
Bad birds come to rest.
A weed turns into a stave.

I remember having a family,
now split and sundered
by greed and secrets.

Now devil's weed shoots past
the declivities.
An old story, the good daughter,
only a child's fable.

I put on cactus skin
thick as chain mail.
One-speared, sister-less,
I hold up the swords of the agave.

Legacy

They covered my mother's farm
with drilling rigs,

knocking down the house
like a stack of blocks.

So we must live now
without the hayfield and the creek,

without the silo, the corncrib,
the orchard, the creek bed.

We will breathe the summery
air only in dreams

where we make soup with water
and bits of stone,

slash the onions
into slivers of regret.

A plume of smoke
rises grimly from the barn.

Since someone has forgotten
to latch the gate,

a thief has entered
the garden,

grabbing the carrots,
ripping onions from their beds

while we watch from
our distant dwelling,

dreaming the past
still exists,

floating on its raft
of broken bread.

Hunger

Dough was made by flour
and salt in the shape of change,
cabbage chopped with fury,
the grape pressed and shrunk.
The dumb hand shovels and
the mouth chews. All we make
becomes comfort or grief. It sizzles
and takes shape, sacrificed

and sliced, arranged, for
we are all tongue and fierce teeth
across the new thing, sure of appetite,
for morning glory, wild sprouts, sweet wine
and sugary death. In us the impossible
wheel of hunger rises and turns.

Dining Room Overlooking the Garden (The Breakfast Room)

—after Pierre Bonnard

It reminds me of my family.
Only half the table spreads beneath
the window: glass of wine, pyramid
of plums, pottery bowl, and creamer
arranged near a basket of bread.

You'd expect the whole table.
And why does the blue-striped cloth
fold toward us as peonies scatter
along the wallpaper like firecrackers?

My mother stands there
in the shadows while Father
slumps in a chair, his face turned
away toward the window.

He's grown tired of domestic
detritus, the artillery of leaves,
claustrophobic battles of mothers
and daughters among china platters.

Beyond the narrow room stretches
the storm cloud of his nearing death.
Soon the table will tip and crumble.
Death's hand hovers over pears.

Childhood Play

We built our hut from
the cemetery of the linen closet.

Like minnows, we dove
into swells of pillows.

We loved, we sang, we played.
We slept. We nibbled popcorn

and peanut butter crackers.
The roof of our tent was

draped with a paisley wrap.
Inside there were layers of comets

on a red backdrop, a courier
who came and announced dinner

for which we had no appetite.
We were cozy there and hidden

from intruders. We could not see
the changing leaves or rime ice

frosting the window glass.
Outside our kingdom

the clatter of plates, the scrape
of knives and forks echoed,

the hum of an engine rumbled.
Beyond the hut lived

tidal waves and typhoons,
missiles, and spy planes.

Sputnik passed the moon.
Riots exploded in Montevideo.

Now my brother is five years gone.
I see my sister rarely.

The hut is gone, and the porch
that held the hut, and

the countryside surrounding,
the row of poplars lining the road,

and that world of play and secrets,
worlds of mystery,

gone, like the gardens
of healing herbs and flowers.

Blackberries

hung from the spiny branch:
My sister and I
pulled them from bushy nests
onto our tongues, tasting
the iron silt of seeds.

Blue-green thorns
pricked our hands.
Juice stained our fingers.
We savored the dark perfume
as we gathered fruit
for preserves, poured them
into glass jars with
tight, shiny lids.

I feel those seeds inside
the jam spread on my toast.
In my sister's house in the cold
basement, the berries wait

like our broken trust,
never returned to sweetness.
All these years, sister,
we have not spoken.
And still, I'm hungry
for your company.

Ontario

Kerosene lamps shone in the dining room
above oil cloth near the photo of the Prince of Wales
and Wallis Warfield. The house balanced on its rocky perch
above the lake. A touch of nobility graced

the mantel—the head of a giant moose.
The Ouija board's alphabet hoped for a happy future
and the living room's Adirondack desk
held a birch bark basket of a beaver,

its mysterious visage hoping for signs of a happy future.
Made by a local Indian woman, her face patterned with scars,
the birch bark basket of a beaver was pieced together
from porcupine quills and sweet grass.

The Indian woman whose face was patterned with scars
belied the image of the beaver atop the basket.
Its porcupine quills, woven sweet grass and clear thread
were things of beauty in her broken shack.

The image of the beaver covered the top of the basket.
When I opened it, the smell of Canada rose: pine smoke and grass.
Invisible threads bound this basket inside her broken shack.
The woman toiled as we all toil, to make love visible.

The basket smelled of Canada, pine smoke and sweet grass.
When I look past all that's been lost, I see this one small thing
that lives along the road of my mind, inside its broken shack
above the lake that endures, far past the northern cities.

The Great Lake

We vacationed on it.
You could not see across.
We floated, we smelled
the heavy hydrangeas
hung from thin stems
on its shores, watched
pine boughs bend and sway
in rainstorms and sunshine.
We read Nancy Drew mysteries
and swung in the hammock,
rowed our canoes across it
watching summer clouds
turn into fierce storms.

Black clouds sometimes appeared
that looked like mushroom bursts
of atom bombs. Ripening blueberries
darkened in the sun. When we dropped
our fishing lines from the dock,
tiny minnows swarmed in schools
among weedy plants at the bottom.
Shouts of joy, tear-stained shrieks arose.
Father scraped and cleaned the fish we caught.

I learned to know it, my lake,
its rocks and shallows, the fault lines.
When I left each September,
it remained large in my mind.
Do you remember the lake of childhood,
the parents gone off in their boat
to catch bass or pickerel?
Perhaps my lake is your lake.
Perhaps you too recall
wild blueberries and sunfish,
water lilies scattered across the cove.

Along the shores of the lake,
wild geese lift and pine trees
slip into the water and we know it
as not a Great Lake but only
our lake where we small birds landed.

Buckeye

In the woods below the road,
I liked to sit on the end
of the branch of the buckeye tree,
scratchy, hard to get to,
full of knots & twigs & burls.
I smelled the soft moss,
watched the bubbling creek
& heard the shouts of boys
riding their bikes,
a rabbit rustling in the ferns.

I was happy to be alone,
to hold the spiky chestnut grenade
polished as a mahogany piano,
clean & smooth with no cracks,
to be away from the scolds of adults,

to live in the silence of leaves,
the solemn eye of the fruit,
peeling its skin back to a white core of heart
above a jungle of weeds beneath
a low branch, far from drunken Hans
& egg gathering & Sunday prayers.

Even now I can smell grass
growing and leaves turning rusty
& know I can summon a train whistle's
lonely shriek or the tap
of a woodpecker's beak against bark.

Cinder

Bitter ash your voice, like a cinder,
your voice like a motor, revving
and roaring and whining, still.
When you were young and penniless,
you sold eggs door to door and made yourself
charming to get what you wanted.
Quarters. Cookies. Sodas.

I let the sheet of memory blow
like flapping linen. Your auburn
hair, high color, deceiving beauty.
Your love of pottery, stacks and stacks
of dishes, bowls and cake stands
cluttering the farmhouse sills, those
childhood rooms we never leave.

Many thresholds I crossed to arrive
at forgiveness. Now that you are gone,
I burn the wood of my anger. It turns
into cinders like the great fire we set
to destroy the coats for your rug braiding.
The flames entwine into the air, disappear.
You're no one. Nowhere.

October: The Farm Is Gone

In this month of shadows,
season of burning leaves,
backlit specks of dust fall like ash
along the living room floor.
A pyramid of apples sits
on the granite counter.

How do we travel from here
as our lives circle and whirl
into black stalks of trees? We fool
ourselves that the stars have
meaning. As we watch autumn
happen, we want more hours,
more months, more years.

October's sign is the scales,
not ones that make a fish's
body smooth and glistening,
but the emblem of a goddess,
severe in her gown,
holding the balance that weighs,
in one bowl the heft
of coins, the other
a fistful of air.

Freight

A woman's thoughts,
she wears them like a harness.
The horse carries its weight
into midnight's darkness.

Seckel Pear

Oh buttery sweetness, slope of musky pleasure,
the tongue's preoccupation. There's nothing
like it in the world, nothing like its smoky shadow
traveling the knotted branch. Nothing

falls with such a slow-spiraled thud
into the wet blades or curves with such
elegant promise among cow hooves
and crow feathers. Before the worm's advance

nothing glows with such sugary flesh or sleeps
so intent and diligent, in its soundless bed.

II

Dear Tomato

No need to frighten me
with your hard ripe heart
and your stem that mimics
the twisted world.

Someone could throw you over
the fence like an enemy.
You could be sliced in half
or fried in butter.

You could be carried into the forest
inside the mouth of a fox
next to whose beating heart
you too would thump and clamor.

Kindergarten

The door's blurred pane
frames the little Evans girl
who screams and struggles
as her mother brings her to the room.

Mrs. Whitehead guards the door,
her spectacles perched
on her nose below tight curls.
Behind her small children sit,

grim and speechless at their desks.
The child clings to the raft
of her mother's leg, then
urine trickles down her calves,

dampens her socks, stains her
new red leather shoes.
I bend my head over my desk
to hide my face. The girl, sobbing,

kicks Mrs. Whitehead's
shin. The teacher pries her
from her mother's hands,
leads her to an empty desk,

helps her into her seat
and restrains her there as we
all hold our breaths, having
crossed this threshold into
a territory no parent can enter.

River of Mantises

I watched a jar once
erupt into a river of mantises.
A blowsy afternoon. Grade
school. Pennsylvania.

The sugar-spun egg case hung
inside a jar from a twig.
We stared at its blankness.

Then suddenly, there
in the middle of math class
asleep over multiplication,

we woke to a jitterbug
of foaming bodies
that bubbled up

from the hardened froth
into a pale volcano
of sticks with giant ivory eyes.

All those bodies poured
out of the jar
down the windowsill

scampering over books
and crayons onto the floor.
When someone opened the door,

we all streamed,
a tangle of jumping legs,
thin arms, into a field,

to watch the mantises
tumbling into the green.
We followed them,

the tiny soothsayers,
prophets of possibility.
We went to

follow their hunger
into the wild,
devouring world.

Montana

Aspen, arrow root, agate.
Bitterroot, bear grass, barking squirrel,
Camas, Clark's nuthatch.
Devil's club. Deer Lodge, Drummond,
Eye of the needle. Emigrant weeds.
Finch. Fireweed. Flatbow people.
Glacier lilies among gray wolves.
Happy birthday, lover of
Indian paintbrush while
Just another June sends endless rain along the
Kootenai. Of silver glaciers,
Lewis's woodpecker I sing. Lost Creek.
Magpie. Malachite. Mountain bluebird.
Ninebark. Nine Pipes.
Oregon grape scatter along the outcropping.
Polebridge, you skirt paradise within paradise.
Russian sage. River of dust.
Self-Heal. Shasta Daisy.
Thirteen moons shine on Two Medicine.
U-shaped upwelling valleys encircle
Valier, Victor,
Wolf Point, anywhere west of the Divide.
X on the gravestone, X on the deed.
Yenne Point, Yellowstone mist.
Zen mountain after Zen meadow after Zen stream.

Thinking About St. Agnes

I can still see her
in the prayer book,
racked and stretched,
burned with live coals.
The nuns of my childhood
spoke of self-denial
and little else during
the long season of Lent.

The only way to prove
faith was through mortification
of the flesh. Only the most
virtuous could exist at
those levels of suffering.

The virgin Agnes,
happy as a bride,
was dragged through the streets
naked. Her hair grew
to cover her. Those who tried
to rape her were struck blind.

The game has gone on
for centuries, the marring
of bones and skin.
Sharp reeds beneath fingernails.
Torn flesh of gallows,
knife and gun.

But why you, Agnes,
head tilted skyward while
a fire began to burn
beneath your small white feet.

Oh Agnes, why turn
into a wisp of smoke?
Why become the ideal gone awry,
pure and faceless,
wanting God while God looks on?

Avalanche

I have been afraid to touch this book,
this volume of stories.
When I do, I smooth my hand across
the white expanse of cover,

I follow the crisp black letters,
and a fear overtakes me
like the panic before an avalanche.

This is a landscape
whose immanence turns
to ashes beneath my gaze.

Packing Up to Leave

In the late afternoon
I stand naked
at the window
to gaze across
the moody lake
a final time—
the pines, the low,
leaden clouds,
a rumpled blanket
with the imprint
of our bodies
across the bed.
A desire to leave
and a wish to stay.

We place white sheets
on the couches.
I peer into the mirror,
but the mirror's gone,
and the cupboard's emptied
of glassware and crockery.
A slant of light crosses
the counter of black granite,
like a crack
in its polished sheen
through which I fall.

Ode to My Lost Quickness

Once I was as quick as a wink,
a flea on a hot griddle,
a flash of flesh

speeding through a small town
on a hummingbird's whir.

If you closed your door,
I'd already be inside
counting the seconds.

People mistook me for
a lightning strike, a flicker's leap,
a minnow's flashing tail.

Quickness—not all it's said to be.
Now I'm glad to be
slow as reeds under the pond.

Now I hold my tongue,
I take my time
and ponder.

I deal with what I have.
No longer the swiftness
of a wing through air,

I am amber inside a rock,
a little something born to disappear.

When I See Crows

Their feathers like
black whiskbrooms,
                racketing into the woods,

they make me think
of endings, the final
flight of a jet,
                the last amber fish in the sea.

Think of all the resurrections
that will go unnoticed,
a tadpole's eye,
                an ivy's tendril, a nascent fin.

When I see a flock of crows,
I think of all we have to say
to each other that goes unsaid,
                words caught in the branches.

The crows could knock them free,
words of love or forgiveness,
expressions of humility.
                Stay with me crows. Tell me again

how you fly, quick birds,
as arrows above
                storm-lashed lakes.

The First Time

In a doctor's office,
the doctor with a flushed face
and liquor breath and no nurse,
and my mother in the waiting room.
I showed him the torn flesh
of my knee where I'd fallen,
the pebbles lodged under skin.

He asked me to take off my blouse.
I did what the doctor said.
Twelve years old. Embarrassed
by my newly formed breasts
that felt like small soft mountains.
He brushed his hand across my nipples
before he moved on
to my torn knee, the memory of him
still lodged like a dark pebble
under my skin.

Bethel Road

If I go back, I expect that everything
will have been kept exactly the way it was
when I lived there, Rose of Sharon flanking

each side of the porch, the little dogs wagging
their tails to greet us, a plaque with Father's
Northern Pike above the door in the breezeway,

the window seat where I imagined I saw a woman
with white braids beckoning the sunbeams.
If I go back, the ghost of my child self might

be alive among the cut glass bowls and
waxed fruit or somersaulting across the roof
of our Cape Cod, spinning with the weathervane.

When I studied at the kitchen table, I spoke
the names of Tanzania and Egypt aloud and wished
that I could travel there. I remember how the people

on our side of the street despised those on the other side
and gossiped until evening came and we left our porches
where we had clustered among flimsy wicker chairs.

Then we sat with our iced drinks and stared at
the blue-black darkness of the television screen.
A dog licked its feet and dozed. I try to remember

what brought us to our beds to sleep, what woke us
at dawn along the usual routes and moved us forward,
emptying the old rooms where others rose up to take our places.

III

Being a Female

I am sick of my hair and my lipstick,
my mascara and eyeliner.
so tired of my eyes, tired of my breasts
and my unspoken comments, tired of
my small footprints and the bandage over my mouth.

I am tired of men repeating my remarks,
pretending they were theirs.
I don't want to be a calf shut in a stall
waiting for slaughter,
a petroglyph smothered in a slab of granite.

It would be exciting to stab a shoe salesman
or paralyze a make-up artist.
It would be marvelous to ride an Arabian
stallion down Main Street,
while wearing a fringed jacket and cowboy hat,
opening my shirt for the world to see.

In the faint corners of photographs,
There I am, hidden in shadows,
stirring a pot, holding a small screaming baby
as birds fly out from the trees like desperadoes.

From now on I refuse to be a frail flower,
a petrified blossom, a rug that everyone
treads upon, lying still and miserable,
waiting for the next heel print.

I will grow smaller and smaller,
a hyphen, an afterthought,
a piece of lint fallen behind a pillow,
a woman who is no longer a female,
finally erased.

I Am Tired of Being a Wife

—after Neruda

I walk into the kitchen stores empty of desire
for Dutch ovens, silicon mats, tart pans.
In the grocery stores and farm markets
I am cold and still as an iceberg.

Recipes bore me. Bathtub rings disgust me.
The smell of bakeries brings me to tears.
I want no more dust rags or oven cleaners,
no more spray starch or furniture polish.

I want to swim in the cool lake of indifference.
That's why the days unroll like heavy carpets
covered in dust and dog hair, bearing
discarded seeds and crumbs,
the lost nickels and pennies.

I only want to slip
like a grain of sand into the ocean.

Seeking the Father

If I were a man, I would wear what he wore,
green work pants and a plain white t-shirt,
sensible shoes. I would go the hardware store
for threepenny nails, a socket wrench, a drill.

When I hear my father speaking, he is saying,
Forge ahead. Thatta girl. Good work.
It is work that binds a family, mowing the lawn,
placing oil somewhere under the hood of the car.

It was not my place to know these things, why
the oil and where it went. So why couldn't he manage
my mother, reckless and high strung, humming like
some motor revving out of control?

The mystery of the father, silent and powerful,
the way he was awestruck by his volatile wife,
punished by his angry mother and sisters.
In the world everyone wears a mask.

Beneath his hid insecurity and the shards of jealousy
which would not succumb to his skillful hands.

Sisters

It began at home,
every morning a breakfast of scorn,
every evening a banquet of disapproval.

Mother insisted we share our
Sunday hats, leading to a fight
each week before Church over
the black velvet tam with rhinestones.

We were fed a diet of competition,
the other female as enemy
because everyone loves a top dog
and what we were was show dogs
in spangled collars, sleek greyhounds,
Pomeranians with tiaras.

And I have been guilty myself
of not speaking words of praise,
not showing up for parties,
offering only a snide word about
a dress badly chosen,
a meal served cold.

Why rivals and sharpshooters
but not friends?
We circled in that
endless show ring,
led on a leash by a strict mother master
while we pranced and pivoted,
let the judge run her hands
over our teeth and our bellies,
lift our legs and pat our hair.

We circled and preened
in the tiny spotlight of our fame,
unable to join together
and cut that leash with our teeth.

The Smell of Workmen

I love the smell of workmen,
cigarettes and soap,
a faint whiff of grease.

I love the way they hum
while they work,
lips pursed in concentration.

I love the sounds they make,
the groans of effort,
gutturals of frustration.

I love their tool belts,
hung with shiny mysterious
implements that look like
silver-winged birds.

I love the way they interrupt
the familiar with
a tap of hammer,
roar of the drill,
scrape of a putty knife.

The cocoons of their hair shine,
lit by flashlights in the attic
as they fiddle
with gauges and dials.

I love their stained hands
and slow sweet smiles,
their sturdy shoes
and broken fingernails.

The way they shed light
on my morning
as they restore things to order,
their work as bright
as flashing knives.

A Memory

In a desert of salt,
gleaming white salt,
one thousand feet deep,
it calls to me
like a buried seed.

What hope this
tiny kernel holds,
an ocean of hopefulness
after the stillbirth,
after the tiny coffin,
and the year of mourning.

This salt calls to
hold the infant,
to bear the child forth
from a thousand feet below.

I cling to one grain of salt
where the eyes, nose, mouth,
birth scream may form again,
exactly as they are supposed to
then appear,
lifted into our arms.

The Right Words

I need to find them,
certain words,
particular syllables.
But everywhere I look,
in yellowed newspapers

and the blue-black dictionary,
under the glossy magazine photos
and tattered envelopes,
they evade me.
I peek under my old stove
and inside my new gloves.

I want to twirl them, swallow them,
send them on errands.
I want to get as close
as I can to the right words,

I want to gulp their wisdom
and eat their sadness,
want to forget the thorny bushes
and dreary blizzards,
to escape
from the mute times.

Tambourines

Tambourines of childhood,
        I hear you thumping
between the drumlin days.

On the wooden stage,
        the children shine
in a ring of light, dancing,

dancing and playing flutes,
        clicking their rhythm
sticks against the evening.

And the tiny bells are jingling
        like shiny sins,
the ribbons flutter from the brass
        like promises,

and the grownups are smiling,
        shifting
in their creaky seats.

Protea

Today begins in sunlight and blossoms.
A wing sweeps the desert.
Eggs boil on the stove.

Swords burst from plants.
I am still alive, surprised
at the rattle of the lampshade,

the knocking of eggs in the pot,
a constant drift of buttery blossoms
onto the patio where they're scattered

by lizards. All night, the star
above the rooftop shone like an idea.
Now it's gone. Only once have I seen

a mountain lion backlit, moonlit,
until she vanished into the forest
and became an absence on the night road.

From the remains of stars, new stars
arise. Helium deep in their cores
keeps them from collapsing.

We could so easily fold and die.
Protea: Three red and three yellow,
mutable, with corollas of silver

remind me to watch as something
luminous approaches, as something changes
before my startled eyes.

The Hardware of the Brain

You might suddenly be in the middle
of recalling it, the word you can't remember,
a word to finish the end of a sentence
in an ordinary conversation and you don't
know where it could have disappeared
so quickly around a corner when you
turned your head, into some dark tunnel
past the bright buttons waiting to be pushed,
the cold steel drawers lined up and labeled so carefully,
lost among the glittering ancestors of thought
pulsing their messages over and over like water
through pipes down the long roads, pushing through,
trying to find its way past the tractor trailers
and the taxis, past the revolving cement trucks
and the tilt top cabs. A bird is flying
through the snowstorm. The snow is thick and soft,

and the bird searches for its own tree in the forest.
The leaves are gone. It is so cold here.
Behind each door there is a smaller door and then
an even smaller one. A pair of feet runs
through the doors. A cat pushes itself over
the fence and leaps through a window.
The window closes. Look in the closet.
Look in the drawer. Look under the bed. No one
can find it. We are all calling. Time to come,

come now. Dinner is waiting. The candle is in
the window. An empty plate waits on the table
next to the folded napkin and glass of milk.
A message is about to be put in an envelope.

Wires are intertwining, about to connect
to longer wires. The fingers touch the keys.
The keys touch the wings. The bright wings
are flapping upward. Wheels are revolving.
Sparks are flying. In this cold and brittle landscape,
someone is trying to start a fire.

Surrender

Rogue seedlings flank
the front bank.

Aspen roots lift
asphalt
from the driveway's face.

I can hear
growth

like a crackle
of flames.
I watch a frantic

squirrel hoard
pinecones,
strip them clean.

Weeds choke the garden,
thorns and buffelgrass.
Wild blackberries seethe.

I scrub green moss.
Still it spreads its stain

across the deck and
falls into cracks where
green sprouts flare up.

I fight against surrender but
the trees call to me
as they creep forward.
The forest wants to take us back.

A Long Marriage

I was the rose and you were the bee.
I was a wolf, you were the bear.
You were the train, I was the tracks.
I was the apple, you were the teeth.
You were the bed, I was the blanket.
I was a riddle, you were the answer.
You were the toast, I was the butter.
I was the hook, you were the fish.
You were the fish, I was the water.
You were the water, I was the lily.

We floated the pond, we soaked in the wind,
soft white against soft dark,
the bones and the flesh,
the midnight feast.
We were the snow falling,
the leaves budding
in afternoon rain.
The fallen, the risen,
the fire and the ash.

Every Manner of Crooked Stem and Thorn

Here, next to the dry arroyo,
I savor the desert in spring:

slow mornings of chattering quail,
dew on the fishhook, hairs sharp white.

Silhouettes of saguaro rise, green and skeletal,
next to devil's claws, javelina tusks,

whiptail lizards, and cactus saddles.
Orange blossoms flare from the tips of ocotillo,

hedgehog cactus aflame with purple fire,
hummingbirds nosing the euphorbia.

I never tire of the modernist sweep of Phainopepla,
like women revving their gray motorcycles.

I watch a gilded flicker
perch like an enlightened thought

on the high branch among hairy
thorns, lime and scarlet blossoms.

I love the desert asleep, its black springs
hidden in the canyons among agave.

I love the desert awake, the smell of
creosote rising after a mountain rain,

the sky streaked with a utopia of branches,
hard and gnarled, difficult with bees,

all its oddness highlighted
like bones under the X-ray's glare.

A carpet of gold unfolds beneath the palo verde tree,
mesquite and ironwood erupting in neon,

the desert opening its arms to bobcat, rabbit,
every manner of crooked stem and thorn.

The Border

As I sip my morning cappuccino,
I think of a small boy setting out
from his village near Oaxaca.
He wants to find a new home.

As I watch patio flowers bend in the breeze
and lift their heads to the morning sun,
that boy rides in a boxcar through a tunnel
clutching a scrap of paper with a telephone number.

I spoon my poached egg, pour my juice.
The boy jumps out of a Ford pickup
filled with hay. Do not fall behind,
says the Coyote. *I will have to leave you.*

Across the wash from my patio, sprinklers
from the golf course fan silver confetti.
Through the thicket, he crawls with his backpack,
brushing off a swarm of fire ants.

As he approaches the muddy Rio Grande,
a child's life jacket dangles from a mesquite branch.
Smells of creosote and rotting fish. Half
a dry tortilla all that's left.

In my yard a cactus wren stops to rest on a lounge chair.
All day that boy follows the shadows.
Peligrosa, he whispers at the sound of a footstep.
All night as I sleep a hundred miles north,

that boy crawls through the desert,
that boy in the gulley,
the border between us.

Kingfisher

Not the oil painting of a tipi at sunset nor
the line of braves on horseback draws me.
I choose the print of a Plains chief, Kingfisher,
whose eyes like the eyes of my father
look out everywhere.

From the bonnet, ermine tails and breath feathers
hang. A stuffed kingfisher sleeps. Attached
to the brow band is a bird you nearly
don't see because it blends into the woven trim
of beads and deep tan hue of the chief's skin.

To be elegant yet unnoticed was my father's way.
All day he would sit on a perch in his boat,
casting a line into the glassy lake. After hours
of watching, he would lean into the tug of line,
hook a fish, haul it up from the deep
and hold it, as I hold this memory, in the calm
radiance of the chief's gaze, and savor it.

My Granddaughter's Face

When I stare at that
strange ethereal flower,
I wonder how she chose
my daughter's body
for her entry into
this world. She could

have been a monkey
or a hummingbird,
could have chosen
the rainforest or
a volcanic island
for her home.

I watch her cornflower eyes,
mysterious eyelashes,
trace the contour of her face,
shaped like my husband's
with his high forehead
and alert gaze.

Gardeners dream
of a flower like you, Adela,
unfolding before them,
a creamy, heart-shaped blossom
uttering birdlike syllables.
The features of our ancestors
are filigreed on your skin.

Sixtieth Birthday

I am an interruption between
the cradle and the coffin.
A quick wink of nothingness.

Here are my antecedents:
cotton candy, blacktopped roads,
rosary beads, a barn with a tobacco poster.

Queen of nightmares, deliver me.
Constant effort, free me.
Starlings, come back to me

because I remember how deer heads bled
beneath buckets in the barn, how
grandmothers lectured me
in a strange language.

I was a ship inside a bottle
among warning buoys,
no lighthouse in the distance,
only the paper waves and sinking clouds.

Sea of Cortez

A flotilla of pelicans
rings the rocky shore.
Their hundreds of
sword-shaped beaks
point to the east

where the pink fizz
of dawn rises.
Below it, a sudden
boil of fish
appears and
stirs the sea.

Silver bodies leap
and thrash along
the water's rim
in glittering heaps
and the pelicans
descend.

I imagine the day
ahead, picture each
pleasure that I wish
to consume,
swimming and sex,
tequila and shrimp,
to devour just as
the birds do.

The birds plummet into
the sea's dark silk,
scoop up their fill
before water goes
dark and the quicksilver
fish are gone.

IV

Leaving Montana

The new owners bought everything:
my bed, my sofa, my oak table,
the chestnut pie safe
in the breakfast room,
even my forks, my spoons.

My body drives south
in a rented van,
into a landscape
of thorny plants.

Here in the desert,
surrounded by ocotillo
and a chain of mountains,
I hear the wails
of coyotes at night.

Stunned by the heat and light,
I am a stranger.
I hear a mourning dove's
syllables at dawn.
I will bend and change
with the new shapes

while my shadow
gazes at what I left behind:
the iron gray lake
and somber pines,
a part of me that still
wades the rocky beach.

Ode to a Mesquite Tree

I never water you
and you stay durable and strong
though the wind lashes your branches
and bees forage your blossoms.

There is something I wanted to ask
about why you don't mind
growing crooked limbs
or having your seedpods plucked
to cure pinkeye.

How wrong that they call you
"devil tree." Your pods
yield a balm
used to heal wounds
and banish headaches,

yet javelina ignore you.
Gardeners toss your limbs
into the ravine. Your name
changes: "honey," "velvet," "screw bean."
Though you are armed with sharp thorns,
you become bread and jelly and wine.
We have needed you for centuries.

Can I, too, transform,
reach forward like one of
your twisted branches, your deep taproot,
and accept my lack of form,
my sturdiness?

My Self-Confidence

It shivers like a wild
compass needle, flicks,
then turns
in the wrong direction

toward our Labrador,
swivels, bumps into
the fireplace grate
and stops.

I open the patio doors,
take a broom
to prod it along
across the ocean of tiles
to the doorsill,
then outside.

I push the tiny flash
until it flings its
crooked self

into the air and leaps,
a wobbly craft
that rights itself
and lands

under a spiky shrub,
camouflaged in green leaves,
changed into a sword,

all scales and tail
and lidded eyes,
a pale green question mark.

Out of Balance

The scales of Libra can veer,
sometimes laden, sometimes filled with air.
My days swing in circles,
from giddiness to despair.

I flutter. I vow. I bend softly
then burst with prickles. As soon
as dread has gone, I'm all ecstasy.
What I can count on is vacillation.

I tilt and swerve, I fly towards
a sky that spins and tumbles.
I hop across stepping stones
moving on a lava flow. I fumble.

My crib was lined with slippery sheets.
Even my death bed will shake with indecision,
my body wanting to slide into its soft nest
yet leap out, ride the animal to the finish.

Sunlight Passes

Sunlight passes through
the lattice of the canopy,
everything luminous as an aurora borealis
or the flickering mind.

Take a moment to drink it in.
You don't have to be the night tourist,
separate, in a state of stasis.
You can wait for the rain for decades,
surrender yourself.

Inside the garden you'll find
a lavender wall,
the pruned crowns of four mesquite trees.
Your eyes zero in on the sky's shrine
where sunlight passes through
the lattice of the canopy.

The rain will appear and
you won't have to be the night tourist
in love with eclipses,
the undersides of clouds.

One by One: Gambel's Quail

One by one they cross, the quail mother
and her thirteen trembling offspring.

One by one they hustle and scatter
and stop our car in its tracks.

They jump the curb and disappear
among the Saguaro, into the thorny wash.

Creosote leaves shudder at their approach.
A bobcat stops, entranced, to watch.

One by one they are eaten by coyote,
or saved, or they step into the Rillito

and sip the ribbon of water, nibble
seeds along the dry wash creek bed.

One by one they parade like squat
drunks with pompadours and crests.

They scuttle and peck, short-sighted,
short-tailed, short-lived. When I look

at them, I want them to stop fluttering
like the pages of a wind-blown book.

I want them to stop quailing,
to step from behind agave shields

and make a high and sudden flight.
Cracks of monsoon thunder

would come from their wing beats.
They would wear battle dress

with a conquistador brandish,
helmets with plumage lifted,

faces painted with stripes, as
lightning branches crackle and flash.

Empty Storefront

No, not a mirror but a city
full of shadows and post offices.
Not a city, but a store window
where wigs wait on pedestals.
No wigs. The shelves of hats,
decorated with fur and rhinestones,
sparrow feathers, smoky grapes.
The pianist sits in her dress
of moth wings. She remembers
that tune about a grassland snake,
the one where a mad barber cuts.
She remembers how the sky opens,
how the trains were no nearer
each time they advanced,
how the night sand slid
blackly into more night sand.

Mission of San Xavier del Bac: Waiting for Signs of Providence

Only the good of heart, claims
the sign, can raise the saint's head.
The Yaqui farmer in line before me
removes his hat, puts his rough hands
beneath the saint's neck to lift Xavier's
head which ascends from its pillow.
Photos of dying children pinned
on his robe shake and flutter.
The worker adds more effigies,
scribbled notes, sad-eyed photos
that protrude like hope with thorns.
St. Francis's own right arm, severed
at the elbow, traveled after his death
to Rome to serve as a relic. Now the good
of heart can still imagine his body whole.
The migrants sob, lift and lower
his head and whisper petitions.
How can one robe weighed down
with such wishes not sink?

Shirt

I bought something new today
that I know I'll grow tired of.
I hang it in my closet with
a pearl necklace at its yoke.

Next to it hangs a coat that was
once my favorite, that I was
once thrilled about and now
will pack away for Goodwill.

The ceiling fan circles and covers
its same path, like my desire for
novelty. I suppose that somewhere
a baker making pastry

rolls his dough then cuts it with
a fluted wheel into a pleasing shape,
bastes it with butter and bakes it,
powders it with cinnamon and sugar.

He knows it will be devoured by others,
say a group of priests at a celebration,
smiling, brushing crumbs from
their worn black shirts.

Of all the things I have
in my closet, this new pin-striped
shirt of lavender linen, with
its flare of skirted peplum,

with its six bone buttons, pleases me.
Its tapered sleeves will carry my arms
in place, its pockets deep enough to hold
my secrets.

Soon

We do not hear the vole
scuttling back to the cornstalk

or the owl drifting silently down
through the branches of the snag.

We do not hear the creatures
with long noses probing the flowers.

We do not hear the border crosser
slip into the muddy river

or the terrorist don her vest
filled with explosives.

We do not hear pollutants at nighttime
escaping into fresh water.

Icebergs slip and crash into the sea,
but we do not hear them.

Even though there are many
things we do not hear,

they still happen and happen.
Will they soon grow loud enough

for us to listen?

Boxcars

The train comes toward us.
Evergreen. Triestino.
The green boxcars.

They're stacked with lumber, carts of toys,
sharp wheels turning
to carry profit for the few.

A train winds like a snake.
Dateland, palm trees, mountaintops
disappear behind it.

Filled with empty boxcars, rattling chains,
the locomotive slows.
Its window holds the emptiness of the world.

A train hurtles toward us
filled with guns, ammunition,
hospital cars, bandages, medicine.

The whistle shrieks and we hear
its piercing bullet.

A train. A train speeds toward us,
the cold nose of a trout.

Smoke and white bones.
We hear the wheels, a click
of flange against track.

It opens its mouth.
The tunnel nears.

Wheels roll on and on.
The lights blink and darken.
The disappearing world.

Amulet

Brown scapular of childhood,
I wore you under my blouse
for protection.

Your soft brown felt enclosed
the picture of the Virgin,
your comforting strings
grazed my skin.
Did I dream you
like some amulet?

You protected me
from lightning strikes,
earthquakes,
men hidden in shadows
behind a pillar.
Without you, now

I'm the stranger who
walks the dangerous world
as armies prepare for battle,

statues tip and sway,
the torches burn
and temples slide like alligators
into the waiting waters.

Happiness: A Painting from the Lost World

The trees are nodding.
The peasants are braiding their hair.
My body leaps up to watch
the deer dancing among
bouquets of daisies
tossed into the air.

We are all joined together
in the drama of endearment.
Whispers of turning leaves,
the buttery moon.
The leaves will turn and turn,
redden, but never fall.

Time stops then flows like water.
Strings and horns. Raindrops.
It is always childhood, always
summer in the green forest.
Once again we are swinging
across the creek on a long vine.

Acknowledgments

ABZ: "River of Mantises," "The Smell of Workmen"
Big Sky Journal: "Montana"
Chautauqua Literary Review: "Buckeye," "Every Manner of Crooked Stem and Thorn"
The Cortland Review: "Legacy"
Crab Orchard Review: "Fable of the Good Daughter"
The Ekphrastic Review: "Dining Room Overlooking the Garden (The Breakfast Room)"
Little Patuxent Review: "Mission of San Xavier del Bac: Waiting for Signs of Providence"
Michigan Quarterly Review: "Hardware of the Brain"
Pittsburgh Poetry Review: "Empty Storefront"
Sliver of Stone: "Dear Tomato"
Spiral Orb: "One by One, Gambel's Quail"
SWWIM: "I Am Tired of Being a Wife"
Tar River Poetry: "Ode to My Lost Quickness," "Sixtieth Birthday"
Under A Warm Green Linden: "Out of Balance, " "Protea," "Surrender"
Your Impossible Voice: "Aileron"

"One by One, Gambel's Quail" appeared in *The Sonoran Desert: A Literary Field Guide*, eds. Christopher Cokinos and Eric Magrane (University of Arizona Press, 2016).

Deepest thanks to my husband, Steve, and to my readers, Natasha Sajé, Connemara Wadsworth, Janet Smith, Tom Speer, Dan Gilmore, Marilyn Halonen, and Jackie Newlove.

About the Author

Geraldine Connolly is a native of western Pennsylvania and the author of three poetry collections: *Food for the Winter* (Purdue University Press), *Province of Fire* (Iris Press), and *Hand of the Wind* (Iris Press) as well as a chapbook, *The Red Room* (Heatherstone Press). She is the recipient of two NEA creative writing fellowships in poetry, a Maryland Arts Council fellowship, and the W.B. Yeats Society of New York Poetry Prize. She was the Margaret Bridgman Fellow at the Bread Loaf Writers' Conference and has had residencies at Yaddo, Virginia Center for the Creative Arts, and Chautauqua Institute. Her work has appeared in *Poetry, The Georgia Review,* and *Shenandoah.* Her work has also been featured on *The Writer's Almanac* and anthologized in *Poetry 180: A Turning Back to Poetry, Sweeping Beauty: Poems About Housework,* and *The Sonoran Desert: A Literary Field Guide.* She lives in Tucson, Arizona.

www.geraldineconnolly.com

www.ingramcontent.com/pod-product-compliance
Lightning Source LLC
Chambersburg PA
CBHW021133300426
44113CB00006B/413